Ghosts

of

Cannock Chase

Terrifying reports of paranormal activity
from the UK's most haunted town

CW01497616

By Lee Brickley

Contents

Introduction

Cannock Chase has been my home for the last thirty-three years, and it is by far the most active paranormal hotspot in the whole of the British Isles. For centuries, local people have reported encounters with spirits, monsters, aliens, and much more. I have written about these sightings extensively during the last ten years, but this is the first book in which I will delve solely into the subject of ghosts.

With a long history dating back to before the Roman invasion, Cannock Chase has always been a thriving beauty spot in which ancient tribes have traded, Kings have hunted, and modern soldiers have been trained.

Situated in Staffordshire, Cannock Chase is a twenty-six mile square idyllic woodland on the outskirts of the town of Cannock. It is home to hundreds of red deer, poisonous adders, and lots of other wildlife, but it is the paranormal happenings that spark the interest of this investigator.

This book contains some of the most creepy and terrifying ghost encounters reported to me by people who live near Cannock Chase woods. Many experts believe the entire area to be a supernatural portal where it is possible to get a glimpse into the next world, and by the time you finish reading this book, I'm sure you'll see there is some weight to that argument.

The town of Hawkins in the popular TV show Stranger Things has nothing on Cannock Chase for sheer weirdness, and no matter how many eerie and unusual events happen here, the reports just keep coming.

The stories in this book were compiled by myself. Being the local paranormal investigator means folks tend to get in touch with me whenever they experience something out of the ordinary, and I have included some of the most freaky and chilling tales in this book.

So, close the curtains, grab a cup of coffee, slide yourself under a blanket, and let's get started.

Oh, and try not to have nightmares!

A Very Cannock Poltergeist

Living in a flat above a shop usually means you are subjected to many unusual smells and sounds during the daytime depending on the niche in which that shop exists. If you spent your time in a dwelling located above a bakery for instance, you'd probably wake up feeling hungry every day due to the pastries being cooked only a few metres away from your bed. If you lived above a hairdressers, you might even have to keep your windows closed during the day. However, nobody really thinks about what might happen at night until it's too late.

Sarah Mills lived on her own and so she rented the cheapest property she could find. She split from her last boyfriend more than six months ago, and apart from going to work, she rarely moved from in front of her television. The flat she rented was directly above a sandwich shop in the village of Heath Hayes, just outside of Cannock.

She would wake every morning to the smell of fried bacon and sausage, but that didn't bother her too much. In fact, she never once complained about a smell during the daytime. It was the ones at night that began to cause a problem.

Sarah had been living in the flat for around three months when she first began to notice something odd happening during the early hours of the morning. She would wake up in her bed and instantly get the strongest whiff of cannabis smoke. Sarah presumed someone was going into the shop downstairs at night and smoking it, or maybe they were even growing it in a backroom or something. After a couple of nights of this, Sarah decided to investigate.

One morning, just before she left for her office job, Sarah nipped into the sandwich shop beneath her flat and approached the counter. She asked the ladies working there if they could ever smell weed, and she explained what had been happening during the night. The ladies were perplexed, and slightly amused, but they were adamant the pungent odor was definitely not coming from their shop. They did, however, agree to check their CCTV cameras in case someone had been sneaking in during the night.

That evening, Sarah arrived home to find a note pushed through her front door.

It was from the ladies downstairs who run the sandwich shop. They explained that the CCTV didn't show anything unusual, and so the smell must be coming from somewhere else. The issue was, there was literally nowhere else it could be coming from. Sarah was confused, but her quest for discovering the truth only strengthened.

That evening, at the same time as the last few nights, Sarah awoke in her bedroom to the strong smell of marijuana. But this time something was different. She couldn't place her finger on it, but she almost felt like she was being watched. All of a sudden, Sarah jumped out of bed and ran towards her living room after hearing the sound of something smashing. It was a photograph of her brother. The frame and glass were both smashed, and the picture lay on her living room carpet.

Sarah's brother passed away three years ago at the age of 33. He suffered a sudden heart attack and never recovered. The doctors said he had some unusual health defect that he'd lived with his entire life. They just discovered it too late to offer treatment. Another interesting thing about Sarah's brother is that he loved to smoke.

Everything fell into place, and Sarah realised her brother was most likely attempting to make contact from beyond the grave.

She did some research online to find out if there was anything she could do to assist her brother's spirit to communicate, and she decided to order a ouija board. It would arrive two days later, but things didn't exactly go according to plan.

Sarah decided she would wait until she was awoken by the smell of cannabis again before she used the ouija board, but right on cue, that happened the following night. Sarah ran into her living room and sat down near the board. She placed her fingers on the glass and said "does anyone want to communicate?" In a flash, three ornaments on her mantelpiece flew across the room, and the glass under her fingertips began to move. The glass spelled out the word "run."

Just then, every door in Sarah's flat slammed shut, and the floor began to rumble. She was worried it was an earthquake, but her logical mind told her this was something paranormal. Sarah, taking advice from the ouija board, got up from the table and exited her flat. She walked down the stairs and into the road in front of the building. As Sarah glanced up at her living room window, she saw what she describes as a demon with horns and red eyes glaring back at her.

Needless to say, Sarah moved out of that flat the very next day. She told her landlord there was a rat problem to avoid losing her deposit, and found somewhere else to live locally.

She now believes her brother wasn't the only spirit attempting to make contact with her. She believes her brother used to smell of cannabis to get her attention, as she knew he loved to smoke, and then warned her just in time about an evil force looking to either take over the space or worse, maybe even possess her.

No matter what the truth might be, Sarah seems to have had a lucky escape.

The Whistling Midnight Miner

It's probably true to say that most people don't spend a lot of time leaning out of the windows in their homes. In fact, you probably only do it to clean the glass a few times each year. However, there is one advantage to being a smoker, and it is that you become far more observant than the average person. You stand around or lean out of windows all the time, and so you notice things. Sometimes those things are good. Sometimes, not so much.

Mike Jones had been trying to stop smoking for about six months, and while he'd been moderately successful, he'd also fallen into relapse a number of times, and this series of strange sightings happened during one of those periods. Mike would manage to last the entire day without lighting up, and then struggle to get to sleep for hours. So, at around midnight each night for a duration of a few nights, he would stand in his bedroom with an open window, leaning out, and puffing away.

On the second night of this particular relapse, Mike had just lit his cigarette when he noticed something strange moving in the shadows at the end of his street. It looked like a person moving towards his position, but he couldn't be sure yet. The figure was yet to move into the areas of the road illuminated with streetlights.

Mike stood there with his eyes transfixed on whatever was moving towards him. Then all of a sudden he began to hear the faint sound of whistling. And at that moment an unusual mist descended on his entire road. The figure came into view. It was a person. It was a man. Mike thought to himself that it was probably someone stumbling home from one of the local pubs, but it soon became apparent his assumption was wrong.

As the whistling figure came into view, Mike could see he was dressed in overalls and was wearing a hardhat. The whistling began to get louder as the figure walked right past the front of Mike's house before disappearing out of view. The mist instantly lifted, and Mike was left standing there with his jaw wide open.

Mike was 100% convinced the whistling man was dressed in the same kit his father used to wear when he worked at the local coal mine, and that made the entire experience even more perplexing.

That mine shut its doors more than twenty years ago.

The following night, Mike stood in the same place at his window in the hope of catching another sighting of the person. He reasoned that if the man was walking to or from some nearby workplace last night, he'd probably do it again. And he was right.

At the stroke of midnight, his entire road filled with mist, right on cue. The man appeared from the dark end of the road, and began whistling as he walked towards Mike's house. Begin the curious type, Mike decided he would go out and attempt to speak to the man to find out why he was dressed like a miner and walking around at midnight. He ran down the stairs and out of the front door.

As he reached the path, Mike began to walk towards the whistling man and soon found himself only metres away.

"Hi, I'm Mike, I just wanted to ask if you..." Mike didn't get to finish his sentence.

The man dressed in an old miner's kit walked straight through him! Mike stood confused. He turned around to shout after the miner, but he had vanished, as had all the mist.

Mike quickly realised he was definitely dealing with a ghost and contacted me immediately.

I did my best to listen to his story and give the best possible advice. I told Mike to get a camera ready this time. To take photos from his window and then run outside as the miner approaches and make a video of the entire thing. He did as I requested the following evening and sent the footage over to me with this message:

Hi Lee

So, here are the photos and the footage from last night. They don't show a single thing. This is absolutely crazy. I could see him clearly when I snapped the photos from my window, and I made a video of him walking towards me, and through me again! But he doesn't show up on that either. This is spooky. I can't believe this is happening.

Sure enough, the photos didn't show any kind of a figure, and the video made Mike look insane. He was attempting to talk to the miner as he claimed it walked through him. But with no miner in the video, it seemed Mike was talking to himself. However, I didn't disbelieve his story. Sometimes spirits refuse to present themselves in photographs and videos.

I also ran some tests on the images and discovered something interesting. If you mess around with the different colour elements on a photograph editor, it's possible to make out the outline of a man. I made the same adjustments to the video Mike sent over and got some amazing results. It's only ever so faint, but if you adjust gamma slightly, there is a definite silhouette of a man wearing a hardhat, carrying a shovel!

It took a few days to get the best-possible renditions, and I wanted to do that before sending them over to Mike. I let him know he wasn't going mad, and there really was something in the photographs and video he sent to me. Mike informed me that he had waited up the last two nights and didn't see anything. It appeared the miner was a short-lived thing that would not repeat endlessly. I agreed to send the images and video over to Mike for him to take a look. Just at that moment, my computer froze, my Skype call with Mike ended, and sparks began to fly from my base unit.

Admittedly, I was using a very old machine, but even the best computer specialists couldn't get it going again. I never got to send Mike the altered images, and I lost them completely.

Why didn't you just get Mike to make the same alterations to his originals? I hear you ask.

Well, I did, but here's the weird thing: no matter how we altered the colours or attempted to edit the video and images, we could not make the miner figure appear. It was like he'd been wiped from Mike's originals at the same time my computer was destroyed.

I finally managed to get a new laptop, which by the way, is far more convenient than a desktop in my opinion, and Mike went back to tobacco abstinence. He tells me that he still looks out of his window at midnight in the hope of catching a glimpse of the whistling miner, but he hasn't seen him again yet.

It's a real shame we lost all the evidence though. Was it destroyed in a paranormal attack on my computer system? I probably can't say that for sure. But the fact that the miner is not even partially present in any of Mike's originals certainly presents a lot of unanswered questions.

A Helpful Spirit

On 7th February 1997, Mrs Brown of Hazelslade saw what she claims to be the most frightening sight one evening at the top of the staircase in her home. After getting her daily fill of Coronation Street and Eastenders, the then fifty-six-year-old lady turned off her television, made a cup of tea, and began walking towards the foot of her stairs. Mrs Brown placed her left hand on the banister and raised her head only to see what appeared to be a man standing on her landing facing downwards.

"I dropped my tea on the floor, I was so scared," Mrs Brown said during an interview with me.

"The man was just standing there wearing a thick miner's coat and overalls. I recognised them because my husband used to work down the pit years ago, before he died," she added.

"I noticed that the man was smiling as he looked down at me, and he seemed to be opening and closing his mouth as if he was saying something, but there was no sound."

Mrs Brown then claims the figure standing at the top of her stairs became erratic. He waved his arms around as if he was trying to tell her something, but a second later when the lady blinked, the specter was gone.

"He just vanished before my eyes. To be honest with you, I didn't even think it was a ghost until I saw him disappear. I thought some old crazy man broke into my house. But after seeing him vanish, there is no doubt in my mind I saw a ghost. I just wish I knew what he was trying to tell me."

I asked Mrs Brown if she thought the ghost looked like her husband or any of his workmates. She said it definitely wasn't her husband, and she couldn't really remember what the other miners looked like because it was so long ago. She did, however, have some photos from a work-related party in the 1960s, and she went off to look for them.

Upon her return, Mrs Brown held in her hand a single old photograph, and she stood in front of me completely ashen. Her rosy cheeks had turned grey.

"What's wrong?" I asked. *"You look like you've seen a ghost...again."*

"I think I have," she said with a trembling voice. *"That's him."*

Mrs Brown handed me the dusty old photograph that showed three people wearing shirts at some function. She told me the man on the left was her husband. And after some more quiet thought, she said the man on the right was the foreman at the local mine. His name was Colin. The man in the middle was the figure she saw at the top of her stairs. His name was Bill, and he died in a terrible accident about two weeks after that photograph was taken. A shaft had collapsed and he died on the job.

It quickly became clear that, for whatever reason, Mrs Brown must have been contacted by this man for a reason. She remembered that his widow was still alive, and so she moved across the room to grab her little black phonebook.

Within minutes, the old lady found a number and began to dial.

"Hello, this is Lilly Brown," she said when her call was answered.

"That's so strange Lilly, I've been trying to get hold of you for the last three years," the voice at the other end of the phone replied. *"I was cleaning my loft ages ago and I found a box full of your husband's old war medals. He gave them to Bill to clean just before he died, and I suppose, in all the commotion, they were put up there and you never got them back."*

Mrs Brown, it turned out, had been searching for these medals for over 15 years, and she began to cry at the thought of finally being reunited with them. The ladies spoke for about half an hour, finished their call, and I soon made my departure.

In the case of Cannock Chase, spirit activity is more often than not malevolent. Most of the stories make your hair stand on end, but at least on this one occasion, the ghost of Bill seems to have simply had some unfinished business.

I check in with Mrs Brown every now and again, and there haven't been any more instances of supernatural activity in her home. Hopefully now both Mrs Brown and Bill can rest.

The House on Rumer Hill

There is a house on the Rumer Hill estate in Cannock that locals fear and refuse to go near. Legend dictates that the house was owned by a witch up until a few years ago, and there seems to be some truth in that story. Although maybe she wasn't a witch in the traditional sense of the word. There was however, a frightening old woman who lived in that house for many years. How do I know this to be true? Because I saw her myself, and so did many of my friends.

The first time I ever heard anything unusual about the lady who lived in that house was around 2008. A good friend of mine had moved onto the Rumer Hill estate, not far from the property in question, and he told me a story one evening that chilled me to the bone. Apparently, following a few drinks in Cannock Town Centre, my pal decided he was going to walk home.

He entered the Rumer Hill estate at the junction with Walsall Road, and was shocked to see an old witchy woman standing in the middle of the road, holding two cats under her arms while she screamed at cars passing by. He told me he believed she was crazy and probably needed some help.

A few weeks later, I told another friend about the story, and he informed me that he'd seen the woman many times. He said she was terrifying and always looked at him with madness in her eyes. He said that something wasn't right about her, and that he wondered what she gets up to in that big old house all on her own.

The house itself, by the way, had a small garden at the front that was surrounded by overgrown bushes. So overgrown was the foliage that it was almost impossible to see the house. It's still that way today. The bushes were so large that they completely covered a small car parked on the driveway of the property. It looked as though the vehicle had been reclaimed by nature.

My sighting of the witchy woman happened when walking to see my father one evening. I always crossed over to the other side of the road when I walked past that house because it gave me the creeps, but this time I felt brave, and so I didn't cross. That turned out to be a mistake.

As soon as I got close to the bushes that surround the house, I began to hear a strange noise coming from them. It sounded like a snarling noise, but it was deep and evil. It was like listening to the hounds of hell. I started to shake and my eyes were fixed on both the bushes and the house, but it was too dark to see properly.

The noise continued to get louder and then suddenly I saw her! Crouching in the garden, behind the bushes, and growling at me. It was the witchy woman! I quickened by pace, completely shocked and honestly terrified. I could see that she was hiding in the bushes, but what really made me scared was her eyes. They were glowing bright red like some evil demon.

That was the one and only encounter I had with the woman who lived in that house. Or so I think...

The house itself appears to have lay empty for the last few years. It seems as though the witchy woman either died or moved away, but it still has the same car in the driveway hidden by bushes, and nothing seems out of place. It is exactly as it was years ago, albeit a little more overgrown.

In the summer of 2019, just before the global pandemic struck, I received a letter from a young local lad who told a rather fascinating story.

He wrote:

Hello Mr Brickley,

I am writing to you today to let you know about something weird and potentially paranormal that happened to me and one of my friends a couple of weeks ago. You know the witch's house on Rumer Hill? Well, we kinda broke into the place and found some really strange stuff. The walls of most of the house are covered in red writing that looks like blood, there's an awful smell everywhere, and three dead cats are nailed to the wall in the hallway. There's a door that I think must lead down to a basement of some kind. I tried to open it, and when I did, I started to hear this snarling sound coming from behind it. Like some sort of wild beast. It terrified me and my friend, and so we left as fast as we could. I just thought I'd let you know in case it was some kind of demon or something.

The letter caught my attention, mainly due to the reference to a snarling or growling noise. It sounded very similar to the sound I heard when the witchy woman was staring at me from behind the bushes in her garden that night. Maybe she was still in the house and she'd just been hiding herself away all this time?

If that was the case, what was all the writing on the walls, and why did she decide to crucify those cats? I had so many questions. I also knew I'd have to go and take a look for myself.

As the boys who broke into the house left in such a hurry, they didn't close the front door properly. That meant I was able to open it a little wider and peer inside without breaking any laws. I lent into the doorway and called out to see if there was anybody home. I then felt a presence and instantly flew forwards into the hallway of the old house. It felt as though someone had grabbed me by the chest and pulled me in there, but I was just not strong enough to resist.

The door slammed behind me, and I was now seemingly stuck inside the witch's house entirely unsure if I'd make it out alive. It was just then I began to hear the familiar sound of snarls, and they appeared to be coming from behind a little door in the hallway. That must have been the basement door the boys mentioned in their letter. I moved towards the door cautiously, reached out my shaking hand, turned the handle and attempted to open it.

The door stuck in place initially, but with a little more effort, I managed to prise it open.

As I did, I felt something brush past me and out into the house. I knew instantly it was the spirit of the old witchy woman. She definitely was not alive and still living in the house, but at the same time, I knew she hadn't left. Every cobweb-covered light in the house then turned on at the same time, and then began the loudest and longest scream I've ever heard. It seemed loud enough to crack the windows, and I had to cover my ears. It was clear I was not wanted in the house. I made my way towards the front door with haste, which opened as if by magic just before I placed my hand on the handle. There was a small notepad on a table by an old telephone, and I don't know why, but I grabbed it on my way out.

When I finally arrived home, I made a cup of tea, opened the notepad, and sat down at the table. The book was filled with rambling and scribbles. It became pretty clear the old woman was, in fact, a witch of some kind. The notebook listed spells for summoning evil spirits, and details for ingredients of potions. It was most definitely a dangerous artifact, and as I read on, I worked out what must have happened to the old witchy woman.

It appears she was attempting to summon an ancient demon who could grant her everlasting life, but something must have gone wrong.

You see, the thing with demons is that you can't always make them do what you want, and it seems the witchy woman found that out the hard way. For whatever reason, the demon refused her request for everlasting life and placed a curse on her that can't be lifted even after death.

She will haunt that house forever. You could go and take a look for yourself. It's easy to find, but I would advise against it. As a paranormal investigator, sometimes it's wise to know when you shouldn't act, and this is one of those occasions. Sure, a priest could bless the house, but the presence there is so evil that I'm not sure he'd make it out alive.

Lots of people still tell me stories of the old witchy woman, but thankfully I've not heard of anyone else attempting to get into the house that is now haunted with her spirit. I hope it stays that way.

The White Lady

One evening in 2001, when driving along a quiet road through Cannock Chase forest, Sam Young had an encounter that he claimed changed his entire life. Sam never believed in the paranormal, and he certainly didn't think ghosts existed until that fateful night. He contacted me in 2006 with this story.

Sam was heading home from a party in Stafford on the evening in question, and it was about 1am. The roads were often pitch black at that time in the quieter areas, and only the light from Sam's car illuminated the area as he drove through. Sam claims he began to feel a strange sensation as he turned a corner not far from the Pye Green area. He felt like someone was watching him, and it gave him the creeps. A few seconds later, he noticed something strange at the side of the road just ahead. It looked like someone dressed in a white sheet, and he thought maybe there were some teenagers playing around and attempting to scare potentially worse-for-wear drivers on their way home.

Sam was intrigued, and so knowing there weren't any other cars around, he moved his car over to the opposite side of the road as he drove to take a closer look. Within a few seconds his car was in line with the white object, and so he stopped and wound down his window to get a closer look. The white figure didn't move, but as Sam's eyes came into focus, he noticed it appeared to be a woman, and she was indeed wearing some kind of white ropes.

Sam shouted to her to ask if she needed a lift, as it was a long way to the nearest built-up area, and there weren't any paths at the sides of the road. He figured it was dangerous to be walking and so offered the lift. It was then the woman turned around to face Sam, and he knew something was wrong instantly. She didn't have any eyes, and her mouth was fixed open as if she was screaming. Without moving her feet, the ghostly woman bolted forwards towards Sam. He describes her as having been floating.

Terrified, Sam started his engine and drove away as quickly as possible. He checked his rear-view mirror but couldn't see anything.

While there are no photographs or direct evidence available, Sam's story is intriguing because of another sighting report someone sent me that happened only a year later.

Derek worked as a lorry driver, and his depot was in the town of Rugeley which is a few miles drive through the Chase away from the town of Cannock. He was on his commute home one night through Cannock Chase in 2002 when he saw something very similar to the specter described by Sam.

Derek claims a woman in a white gown walked out into the middle of the road in front of his car. He swerved to avoid her and ended up crashing his car into a ditch. When he scrambled out of the vehicle and up onto the road to see if the woman needed assistance, she was gone. He called out and looked around, but couldn't see anything.

When the police arrived at the scene with the JCB required to pull Derek's car out of the ditch, he told the officer about what happened. Unfortunately, Derek didn't record the officer's name, and we've been unable to trace him. However, when Derek finished telling his tale, the officer put down his notebook and said something rather interesting.

According to Derek, the policeman said *"You know, it sounds like you saw the White Lady. You're the third person to give me a story like that in five years. I presumed they were all lying but it's pretty incredible you all describe her in the same way."*

What does the White Lady of the Chase want? Nobody seems to know. But one thing is for certain, seeing her often means something bad is going to happen. There are at least four instances, according to the policeman, of people driving off the road when they see her. Sam appears to have had a lucky escape. If you ever see her when you're out driving on Cannock Chase, it's wise to turn around and find another route.

Never Steal

from Dick Slee

James was an average teenager from Cannock who lived in a flat just off the Walsall road with one of his friends. He moved out of home at 16 due to some family issues, but his friend Mat came to the rescue and offered him a place to live. Luckily James already had a job, and so he was able to pay his own way.

A few months after moving into the flat, during an evening of drinking and taking some illicit substances, Mat told his mate James a story about a man who used to live on Cannock Chase. His name was Dick Slee. He was a hermit of sorts, and he lived in a cave on Cannock Chase for many years. Indeed, "Dick Slee's Cave" still appears on many maps of the Chase today, but it's pretty difficult to find.

Anyway, Mat said that Dick Slee lived up there on his own for many years, and locals believe that he was arrested and imprisoned sometime before he died. Apparently Mr Slee survived by quietly sneaking down into the town of Cannock at night and stealing from local residents. He'd been doing that for many years, and eventually the police became tired of the hermit and arrested him. That was how the story went locally anyway. But Mat offered a different ending. He told James that Dick Slee wasn't arrested. Instead, he disappeared altogether, and some people think he was murdered.

James listened intently, and he became almost obsessive about learning as much information as possible. He logged straight onto the internet and searched for the term on Google. He found a few results that all confirmed the mainstream telling of the story. He even found a map that pinpointed Dick Slee's Cave, and managed to convince his friend Mat to go exploring there with him the following day.

It turned out that Dick Slee's Cave, or what was left of it, was located at the Oakedge end of the Marquis' Drive, a popular area where people enjoy barbecues and sunbathe in the summertime on Cannock Chase. There was barely anything left on the site, but checking on the map, James and Mat knew they were in the right place. There was still a small hollow, and James fought his way against brambles to get inside.

The area was cold and damp, and there was a smell James says she would prefer to forget. On the floor, James noticed something poking out of the soil. It seemed to be made of wood. He bent down, moved some earth out of the way, and retrieved the item. It was a carving of a small man with a bent spine wearing a long hooded coat. James showed the item to Mat who suggested they should take it home.

Upon arriving back at their flat, James went to the bathroom sink and cleaned the carved figure as best as he could. He then sat down in the lounge to examine it. Mat leant over James' shoulder for a couple of minutes as both of them examined the piece.

"Maybe it's something Dick Slee made?" Mat said with a giggle.

"Can't be." James replied.

With neither of them being able to work out exactly what the figure was or where it might have come from, they placed it in a kitchen drawer and forgot about it. A few days later, James began to experience strange goings on that we now believe could be associated with the object.

While lying in his bedroom relaxing one evening, James noticed something on the back of his bedroom door. It looked as though he could see a face in the wood grain. He was sure it must have been his eyes playing tricks on him, and so he turned over and faced the other way towards the wall. However, a couple of hours later when he rolled back over, he noticed the face was still there. It was only faint, but he could just about make out what looked like the head of a man imprinted on the back of his door.

A few days later, James mentioned the experience to his friend Mat while they were having a drink, and Mat said he wanted to take a look to see if he could see anything in the door. Both of them went to James' room, switched the light on, and had a look. James could see the face of the man instantly, and this time it seemed far more defined than before. He could not believe it when his friend Mat said he couldn't see anything. The face seemed so clear. It was an old man, maybe in his 60s, and his head leaned forwards so his eyes were looking up from under his eyebrows. Mat couldn't see a thing.

Over the following days and weeks, the face in the door began to become clearer and clearer to James, to the point where he could see the wrinkles on the old man's face.

James thought he might be going mad, but other than the face in the door, he really didn't feel that bad. Then one night things took a turn for the worse.

James was in bed, it was about 1:30am, and he was about to fall asleep after a long shift at work. He saw the face in the door as he entered his room, and it appeared almost like the most realistic portrait painting he'd ever seen. He was still bemused by the fact his friend Mat couldn't see it, but James had also learned to mostly ignore it. He worried that if he was going mad, paying attention to the hallucination would just make things worse. Anyway, he turned out his bedroom light and rolled over. About three minutes later James felt breathing on the back of his neck.

The young man jumped up in his bed and threw his back against the bedroom wall. In front of him was the old man he'd seen in the door for the last few weeks, except he wasn't in the door anymore, he was standing at the side of James bed breathing heavily. James shouted for his friend Mat as loudly as he could, but unfortunately, Mat always slept with earplugs as he would often wake from the slightest of noises otherwise.

The old man from the door spoke. He said in a gravelly voice *"you stole from me,"* and raised a boney finger to point at James.

James says it was at that moment that he noticed the old man was floating above the ground. He didn't seem to have any feet, and if he did, he certainly wasn't standing on them. James thought fast and quickly remembered the wooden figure he took from Dick Slee's Cave. He jumped off the bed and past the old man, ran into the kitchen and retrieved the object. He then threw it into his bedroom from behind the door, too scared to look back into the room and see the old man again.

James finally woke Mat and told him what had happened. Both of them went into James' bedroom to investigate, but the old man was gone. Mat asked James where he threw the wooden carved figure, and they both searched the room for over an hour, but it was nowhere to be seen either.

James and Mat never had any more problems with the paranormal, and the face in the door disappeared, but neither of them are willing to go anywhere near Dick Slee's Cave again, and they both suspect the face in the door and the old man in the bedroom were both Dick Slee coming back to his what what his.

If you want to find Dick Slee's Cave on Cannock Chase, simply search online and you'll find maps that show you exactly where it is.

However, it wouldn't be sensible to go there alone, and if you find anything in the hollow, make sure you leave it there. It's ironic, but the hermit who stole from so many others seems to become rather irate if you steal from him.

Devil Dogs

on the Monkey Trail

Cannock Chase might be known throughout the entire world as one of the most active hubs for paranormal activity, but it's also famous for a few other things, one of them being its many miles of woodland mountain bike trails. People come from all over the UK, and indeed the world, to ride their bikes through the trails at Cannock Chase, and so it should come as no surprise to readers that a lot of those folks encounter strange and unexplainable things.

One such occurrence happened on the infamous Monkey Trail during the spring of 2018. John Wilks arrived at Cannock Chase and parked at the Birches Valley car park before making his way towards the beginning of the Monkey Trail. He went there at least one morning every week as he worked from home and so had the freedom to get out and enjoy the woods early.

He would complete his day's work later on. The Monkey Trail would only take John around an hour, and he would have plenty of time left in his day.

Just like every other time he was there, John got on his bike and began to ride. The morning was uneventful until John's wheel hit a ditch and he was thrown over the top of his handlebars. He fell hard on the ground and injured his wrist, but he wasn't too badly hurt all things considered. The cyclist clambered to his feet and inspected his bike. It didn't look like there was anything more than superficial damage. It was then John heard the noise of growling for the first time. He instantly panicked because he knew it sounded like a dog, and he was not the biggest fan of our canine friends.

John sat back on the seat of his bike and began to ride away, but the sound of growling began to get louder no matter how fast he pedaled. John then started to hear barking. He knew he was definitely being followed by a dog, but it almost sounded like there might have been a pack of them. It was then that John made his second cycling-related error of the day and crashed his bike straight into a tree. He fell to the ground once again and almost knocked himself out.

Dazed and a little confused, John then says he sounds of growling and barking seemed to surround him.

He didn't know where to turn because the sounds seem to be coming from all sides. John then saw what he describes as the biggest and blackest dogs he's ever seen emerge from the bushes. There were around eight of them, although he didn't count at the time. He said they continued to move closer, and as they did, he could see a crazed look in their eyes and spit dripping from their mouths. They looked hungry.

John stood up, grabbed a stick from the floor and began waving it towards the dogs, spinning his body in a circle. He shouted for them to stay back, but they just kept coming. It was then that one of the black dogs leapt forwards and bit a chunk out of John's exposed leg causing it to begin bleeding heavily. John screamed out in pain, and as he did, the pack of wild black dogs seemed to vanish right in front of his eyes. Two seconds later, another cyclist came into view, saw John's injuries, and insisted on helping him back to safety.

I've seen John's scar for myself, and there is no question in my mind it came from the bite of a huge dog. John doesn't go cycling on Cannock Chase alone anymore, but thankfully he made friends with the guy who seemed to scare the devil dogs away on that fateful morning, and now they always complete the Monkey Trail together.

John said he did tell his new friend about the incident that led to him being injured that morning, and his cycling buddy is skeptical but still agrees they should always go together.

Over the years, there have been multiple reports of large black dogs on Cannock Chase, and many of the sightings do seem to have a paranormal element. Where do they come from and why are they so aggressive? Maybe one day we will find out.

Nazis from
Beyond the Grave

One of the most interesting facts about Cannock Chase is that there are 5000 German graves of military personnel from World War 2. When the war ended, the UK government made an agreement with the German government to make it easier for the families of loved ones to visit the graves of the people they lost. As part of the deal, all German soldiers buried in the UK were excavated and relocated to Cannock Chase. Indeed, that is still why the Cannock Chase forest welcomes hundreds of German guests and tourists every year.

However, having so many bodies of German soldiers buried on Cannock Chase should make it come as no surprise that people in the local area report many strange associated happenings. I wrote about a few of them in my first book "UFOs, Werewolves and the Pigman," and you can still get that book online if you want to read more on this topic and many others.

The following story did not feature in that book, but it is so incredible that I thought it deserved a place in this one. I was first made aware of this story in 2016, and it occurred a year prior to that.

Clive and Andrea are a couple from Huntington in Cannock who often take their two dogs for a walk in the forest during the evening time. They usually finish work, prepare and eat their dinner, get changed, and give their dogs some exercise. The following account happened on one such evening.

The couple walked onto Cannock Chase via a small pathway located on the Stafford Road in Huntington. They let the dogs off their leads as they usually did if there weren't too many people around, but unusually, neither of the canines wanted to move too far away from the couple. It was commonplace for them to run off into the trees and play, but for some reason they didn't seem to want to do that on this occasion.

After about twenty minutes of walking Clive and Andrea stopped at a bench and sat down for a rest. The dogs sat beside them, as if guarding the couple from something. It was then Clive claims he saw someone moving around in the trees. Assuming it was just kids having fun, he didn't think too much of the sighting.

That was until the figure in the trees began moving closer and Clive could clearly see it was wearing an old German military uniform. It even had a swastika. Clive turned to his wife and asked her to look in that direction to confirm what he was seeing. Andrea could see it too, and she says she felt very scared.

The couple decided to walk back along the same route and take their dogs home, only to find the figure in the Nazi uniform appeared in front of them and blocked their path. Clive and Andrea froze, and their dogs began to bark loudly at the figure in front of them. The German soldier then started running towards the couple who both closed their eyes. When they opened them again, the soldier was gone, and their dogs were no longer barking.

While this event didn't happen within the vicinity of the German Cemetery on Cannock Chase, it was only a few miles away. Also, it was very near to the area in which there used to be a prisoner of war camp in the forest during the 1940s. Could the soldier in the Nazi uniform have been someone who died at the POW camp, but who's remains were not moved into the cemetery with the others? Very probably. In fact, many experts believe there are Germans buried all over Cannock Chase who did not get relocated due to a lack of information about the position of their graves.

Clive and Andrea say they've never had any other unusual sightings or encounters on Cannock Chase, but they'll never forget the day they saw the Nazi from beyond the grave.

The Black-Eyed Child at Castle Ring

I hit the headlines for the first time in 2014 after publishing reports of a black-eyed child that local residents continued to report on Cannock Chase. I wrote about it all in my first book, but I also published another little book last year that contains lots of different sightings of the black-eyed child that didn't make it into the press. For that reason, I didn't want to discuss the same stories over and over again, but I did want to make sure the famous black-eyed child of Cannock Chase got an honorable mention in this book.

The story I'm going to relay here didn't get mentioned in either of my other books for the simple reason that it got overlooked, and I never followed it up. In preparation for writing the book you're reading right now, I got in touch with the lady who sent me this story and got the full lowdown from her. I'm sure you'll agree, this is one of the most interesting sightings of the devilish black-eyed child to date.

Unsurprisingly, it happened at Castle Ring.

For those who don't already know, Castle Ring is an iron age hill fort that sits at the highest point of Cannock Chase forest. It was once occupied by a Celtic people known as the Cornovii who were renowned for their strange rituals and blood sacrifices. The tribe fled Cannock Chase and were never seen again following the Roman invasion of the British Isles. When Roman soldiers reached Castle Ring in the Autumn of AD42, the site was completely abandoned. However, spooky supernatural reports have been thick and fast ever since, leading many experts to believe the Cornovii people may have placed a curse on the land before they made their retreat. Castle Ring is also the area of Cannock Chase with the highest number of black-eyed child sightings.

Some paranormal researchers lean towards the theory that the black-eyed child is the ghost of a little girl murdered on Cannock Chase during the 1960s. And indeed, there were a number of disappearances and murders of children in the area at that time. A local man called Raymond Morris was arrested and convicted of some of the crimes, but police never managed to find a couple of the girl's bodies. For that reason, some people believe one of the girls haunts the area and has become known as the black-eyed child.

I have a different theory. I believe the black-eyed child to be an evil spirit conjured by the Cornovii tribe to protect their captured land and warn off anyone who dares try to occupy it. It's clear to see from all the stories available online and in the press that the black-eyed child is not a peaceful spirit, and it nearly always causes alarm or even, in some cases, injury.

Anyway, back to the story at hand!

This sighting report was sent to me from Jane Harris, and I think you'll find it fascinating:

Hello Mr Brickley

I just wanted to get in touch with you to let you know about something I saw last night while walking around Castle Ring. I go there all the time because my grandmother's ashes are scattered below the big tree at the back of the hill fort. You know, the one that looks out over an amazing view of the woods?

Well anyway, I was standing in that position talking to my grandmother in my head when I saw a little girl looking at me from behind the trees in front of me. She had a white face, jet black hair, and she looked like she was wearing some sort of old dirty school dress.

I called out to her to see if she had lost her mummy, but she didn't reply. She just giggled and turned around before running off into the trees.

Now I know Cannock Chase well, and I know there is nothing in the direction she ran except for more trees and dense woodland. I decided I couldn't let the little girl run off that way on her own, and so I decided to follow. I picked my bag up off the floor, ran down the hill towards the girl and into the trees. I could see she was about twenty feet in front of me, and she kept stopping, looking at me, giggling, then running again. I just couldn't seem to catch up with her. The next thing I knew I felt an extreme pain in my left foot. I looked down to discover I'd managed to trigger some kind of hunting snare and it had injured me somewhat.

I couldn't continue to run, and the girl seemed to disappear, so I just made my way back to Castle Ring car park and started my engine. I wasn't too badly harmed. I didn't need stitches, but it could have been a lot worse.

When I finally found that email, I got in touch with Jane and arranged to meet her at Castle Ring to go through the encounter and get a better idea of what happened. Jane was surprised to learn it was no shock to me that she became injured on that day.

In fact, in most instances when people see the black-eyed child, she tends to lead them into dangerous places and situations. If they follow her far enough, they nearly always suffer physically. While there are no reported deaths associated with the black-eyed child, plenty of people die on Cannock Chase in the woods, and some of those fatalities could be linked. Maybe they just followed her too far?

Jane showed me the area in which she stood talking to her deceased grandmother, and then we walked off into the trees where she followed the black-eyed child. There was no sign of the creature when we were there together, but we did find something rather unusual and weird. In the exact location where Jane injured herself on the hunting trap, there was a dirty old ribbon on the floor on which the words *"see you next time"* were embroidered.

Maybe it was just a coincidence? Maybe the black-eyed child knew we were coming and decided to leave a message for Jane? Either way, she doesn't go to Castle Ring quiet as often anymore, and I don't blame her!

Creepy Waters

at Pottle Pool

Just north of Huntington, and west of Badgers Hill in Cannock, you'll find an area known as Pottal Pool. The entire site was once a working quarry, but today it's mostly used as a pleasant walking area. As the name suggests, there is a large pool in the area known as Pottle Pool Pit. That is the location of the next ghost story reported to me by a resident of Cannock Chase.

This story happened around Halloween in 2013, and it is perhaps one of the most incredible in this book.

October is a brilliant time to go for a walk on Cannock Chase because the scenery looks so beautiful. The brows and greens really are something to see, and that is why Kevin Donnely decided to spend an afternoon exploring. It was raining outside, and so Kevin put on his waterproof jacket before leaving home.

He didn't mind getting a little bit wet anyway. It was worth it.

Kevin lived in Huntington which is near to Pottle Pool, and he'd heard all about it before but never visited. He used his mobile phone to make sure he was walking in the right direction, and his journey seemed relatively uneventful as he found the famous pool and sat down at the side of it to enjoy the peaceful atmosphere and view. There were a few other people around doing the same thing, and Kevin was in no hurry to get home, even if it was raining.

As the hours passed, Kevin sat there with an empty mind watching the world go by, except he wasn't paying as much attention as he thought. He soon realised that everyone else sitting around the pool had left, and he was the only one there. It was also getting dark, but Kevin thought he'd wait a little longer as he wanted to see how stunning the area would look in the moonlight. He watched the sunset, and just as he was about to stand up and begin the walk home, something weird happened. Kevin heard the unmistakable sound of someone shouting *"heave, ho!"*

His eyes were drawn towards the middle of the pool where he could now see a small vessel that seemed to me emanating a kind of fog. He says it was the most flabbergasting thing he's ever seen. Onboard the boat were two people.

One of them had a pipe in his mouth and seemed to be wearing what Kevin presumed was a captain's hat. The other sat in front of the man rowing the boat at his command. The boat slowly moved into the middle of the pool and then changed direction to return to its original position before vanishing into thin air. Kevin left the area and returned home entirely perplexed with the events that unfolded.

Kevin told me the sailors looked like they were from the 1800s, but the only other thing he remembered was the lettering on the site of the boat. It spelled out "The Quarryman."

We can only presume that must have been the name of the vessel. Kevin returned to the area the following evening to see if he could see the ghostly sailors again and perhaps even make contact, and sure enough, as soon as the sun set, the foggy boat appeared. Kevin said he wasn't as shocked this time, and so he managed to get a better look at them. The "captain" was holding a lantern of sorts, and there was a symbol on his hat. It was a skull and crossbones symbol.

Kevin tells me he tried to get the attention of the sailors, but he was unsuccessful. No matter what he did, the sailors, or pirates, acted as though he wasn't there. And although Kevin went back there again and again, he was never again lucky enough to see them.

However, he did tell me that another local resident overheard him telling someone about it in a pub and added that he had seen something similar. Sadly, Kevin never got the man's name, and so we can't contact him for comment.

Why would the ghosts of sailors appear in a pool in the middle of England? Isn't that a little bit far from the sea? Well, Cannock Chase is a paranormal portal area, and so spirits often appear there having traveled from many other places and dimensions. It just seems, for whatever reason, there are a couple of pirates who've chosen Pottle Pool as their home, and while they're not causing any harm or panic, I don't think that's so much of a bad thing.

The Pye-Green

Hitchhiker

Stand anywhere on Cannock Chase with a decent view, and you're going to be able to see the Pye Green tower. The structure is part of an emergency government communications system that was built during the Cold War, and it was intended for use in the event of a nuclear attack by Russian Communists. The tower is part of a small network of similar structures around the UK that all exist within line of sight. So, from the top of each tower, you can see the next, many miles away.

In recent times, the Pye Green tower has been used by many telecommunications companies including BT. But the original communications equipment is still in place, and the Pye Green tower could theoretically kick back into action if the need ever arose.

The tower itself requires little maintenance, but that wasn't always the way. During the 1960s and 70s one man had the job of caretaker, and he would spend his days working alone at the tower. He was more of a security guard than anything else, and he was tasked with making sure local people didn't break into the site or cause any damage. Sadly, the man died in 1982, and nobody replaced him as the telecommunications system was no longer a national priority.

Right up until his death, the man who guarded the tower would lock up at the end of his shift and hitchhike home. Things were different back then, and most of the people in the local area knew each other. As the tower is in a remote location and the man didn't drive, he would start to walk and then ask for a lift off the next passing car. More often or not he would know the driver. You would think that since his death the man no longer attempts to get a lift home from outside the Pye Green tower, but you would be wrong.

I have personally received no less than twelve reports during the last ten years from people who saw a ghostly figure outside the Pye Green tower holding his thumb out. In nearly all the reports sent to me, the man disappears if people actually stop their cars to offer a lift, but everyone says the man is always smiling before he vanishes. Here is one such report:

Mr Brickley,

I hear you are the person to contact about a sighting I had recently on Cannock Chase. I was driving from the German Cemetery towards the Samson Blewett pub in Pye Green when I spotted this old gentleman at the side of the road, and he seemed to be trying to flag me down for a lift. He looked pretty friendly, and so I thought I'd oblige. I flicked my indicators and began slowing down to stop for him. I pulled over and waited for him to walk up to my window, but he never did. I even got out of the car to have a look around, but I couldn't see him anywhere. My friend says she had a similar thing happen and that you might know a little more about it? Any ideas about this ghost?

I hear the best time of day to catch the Pye Green hitchhiker is around 6:30pm; the exact time the tower guard's shift would finish all those years ago. Perhaps maybe one day someone will manage to pick him up and take him home, although that's unlikely. What seems most logical is that the old man hitched a lift from that area so many times during his life that he left an imprint on the area. What people are seeing is more of an echo of the past than an actual spirit I'm sure, but who knows? Cannock Chase is a weird place!

Chariots at
the Roman Way

It is widely known that a road called the A5 that runs through the town of Cannock is a hotbed of paranormal activity. There are many different stories online and in books about odd and unusual things happening in that area, and it's unsurprising when you consider how much history it has.

The A5 or Watling Street as it is otherwise known is a road first carved out and cobbled by the Romans following their invasion of England. The original road actually ran all the way from Dover to London, and it was then extended through Cannock all the way to Wroxeter (where there are still some amazing Roman ruins today.)

Since it's construction, thousands of people have died along the A5, and it would seem many of their spirits still haunt the area. Indeed, the most haunted pub in Cannock, the Four Crosses, sits along the A5.

If you follow the A5 out of Cannock, you almost instantly come across a hotel that is aptly called "the Roman Way." Over the years, there have been many strange goings on there, and lots of people who visit the area claim to have seen spirits when staying at the hotel. I wanted to mention one such incident in this book, but there are many more, and lots of them are strikingly similar.

Guests who stay in the Roman Way hotel often report the same sighting in the early hours of the morning. Many of the rooms have windows that look out onto the vast car park, and that is where people claim to see the ghosts of Roman soldiers racing golden chariots.

Mrs Stevens sent me this report in 2016:

Dear Mr Brickley,

I visited Cannock Chase last night for the first time in my life. I had to go there for work, and thus required a hotel room for the evening. Tripadvisor recommended the Roman Way as a decent place to stay, and so I made the arrangements and checked in. While there were no issues with the room, something unbelievable happened during the night and I really don't know what to make of it.

Around 1am, I woke up to hear the sound of rumbling outside of my window. I could also hear what sounded like horses galloping around. It was quite surreal.

I got out of bed and opened the curtain to see the most astonishing sight. Please don't think I'm mad, but there were around twenty people in the car park all dressed in Roman attire, and they appeared to be racing chariots. The weirdest thing was, the chariots would race forwards towards the front of the car park and then fade out in front of my eyes. One by one they all vanished. I honestly think I saw ghosts.

I mentioned the whole thing to the lady working at reception before I checked out in the morning, and she said that a lot of people have these sightings, and that I should contact you to log my report.

It really was the most insane thing I've ever seen, but I didn't even have a single glass of wine before bed, and I am quite certain I was awake.

Mrs Stevens' report is quite typical, but sightings of this nature are not strictly limited to the area surrounding the Roman Way hotel. In fact, people report ghost encounters all along the A5, but there's hardly any wonder why.

There are multiple Roman ruins in the vicinity, and the road itself would have been incredibly busy when it was first built in ancient times.

Planes on the Chase

I've written in my previous books about aeroplanes that appear and then disappear on Cannock Chase. Indeed, it was my own father who once saw it happen right in front of his eyes when visiting the iron age hill fort at Castle Ring. He was standing at the back of the fort facing out over Cannock Chase and Rugeley when an all grey military-style cargo plane flew into view. As fast as it appeared, the plane seemed to dip down behind some trees and disappear, never to resurface.

There is a small runway near to Cannock Chase where light aircraft take-off and land providing aerial tours of the local area. However, it is not used by the military for any purpose, and it's probably impossible to land something as big as a cargo plane on such a short runway. Those facts led me to believe from the start that the aeroplane my father saw was something a little more supernatural.

During the early 1900s, the Cannock Chase forest was used as a military training ground for troops preparing for the First World War.

It was used again for the same purpose during the Second World War, and it also became home to a German prisoner of war camp. So, over the years, there were many military craft taking-off and landing on Cannock Chase, which makes it not entirely shocking so many people see unusual planes that seem to vanish into thin air.

This next report comes from David Michaels who saw a similar plane to my father early in 2021:

Hey Lee,

So I was walking on Cannock Chase the other day near the old training camps at Brocton, and I could hear a huge engine getting nearer and nearer. I presumed it must have been a helicopter or some kind of light aircraft, but the engine just seemed so loud that I was a bit startled. Anyway, I looked up to the sky in front of me and saw this old grey plane appear from behind the treetops. It was huge, mate. Truthfully, I've only ever seen planes like that at the Cosford air show. I could see it in the air for about ten seconds, and then it flew behind some trees and I lost sight of it. Wanna know the most crazy thing? The plane was so low that I swear I could see the pilot, and he seemed to be wearing those old-style goggles you see in WW2 movies. Weird eh?

David was right. It was weird, but with so many reports of this nature coming from the locals on the ground in Cannock Chase, it seems reasonably safe to assume there are some old RAF guys out there with some unfinished business.

Although I have researched extensively, I can find no evidence of military craft crashing on Cannock Chase during either the First or Second World War. However, that doesn't mean it didn't happen. There have certainly been enough cover-ups related to UFOs landing in the Cannock forest over the years, and so the sightings of all these ghostly planes only raise more questions. Did the military cover-up a plane crash at some point in the past? What were the pilots of these ghostly aeroplanes doing originally? And why are they still hanging around? Maybe we'll never know, but the sightings continue regardless.

Spirits Moaning
Among Tombstones

While the German war cemetery might be the most famous of its kind in Cannock Chase, there are many other cemeteries dotted around the local area with plenty of weird goings-on as one would expect in such an active paranormal hotspot.

This report relates to one of the larger gravesites in the local area situated along the aptly named "Cemetery Road", just outside the town centre. The site has been used as a place of rest for many hundreds of years, as becomes apparent if you go there and take a look at the carvings on some of the oldest gravestones. I managed to spot one dated from the early 1800's but there are probably some older than that. As with most gravesites, after a few hundred years, graves are reused.
There are many stories circulating in the town of Cannock about spooky and unusual sightings that occur within the walls of the cemetery, but this is by far the most interesting one I am yet to publish in one of my books.

Robin Yates has more than ten different family members buried on Cemetery Road, and he's been going there a couple of times each month since his father died in 1992. Up until that point, his father was the one who tended to the family graves and made sure they were suitably maintained.

On this occasion in 2002, Robin parked his car at the cemetery and made his way down the pathways towards his father's grave. The old man had a large granite headstone that looked well-kept, and Robin had come to lay some flowers. He had also hoped to check in on his other family members before going home to his wife for Sunday lunch.

As he approached his father's grave, Robin saw a lady dressed all in black sitting on the bench closest to his father's headstone. She wore a black veil over her face and her arms were covered with long black gloves. She looked as though she had just been to a funeral, and so Robin didn't try too hard to get her attention. He just wanted to leave her in peace.

However, as Robin approached his father's grave, the woman in black spoke. She said *"he was such a good man, your father."*

Robin turned to face the lady in black who now raised her head a little to reveal her face.

Robin instantly froze and began to tremble. He wasn't certain, but he thought the woman looked very similar to photographs he had seen of his mother when she was in her 20s. Unfortunately, Robin never got to meet his mother because she died during childbirth, as would happen a lot back in those days.

"You're a good boy" the woman in black said, pulling the veil from her face.

Robin could now see without a shadow of a doubt that the lady sat on the bench by his father's grave...was his mother?

"What is going on?" Robin asked the woman in black nervously.

"Oh don't worry yourself boy, I'm just checking in one last time before I head off" she replied.

"Head off where?" Robin inquired, beginning to feel a little more comfortable, but still confused by the entire situation.

"Don't you worry about that. You blink and I'll be gone" the woman in black said.

Robin tried not to blink his eyelids for as long as possible, but the lady disappeared the second he gave in to the urge.

I've done some work with Robin using a spirit box, which is a piece of equipment that scans through different frequencies and can often pick up the paranormal. One two separate occasions our sessions appear to have produced results, and both times Robin has been convinced the messages were from his mother.

Perhaps Robin didn't lose her at all? Maybe, just maybe, his mother has been watching over his shoulder this entire time, keeping him safe and guiding him? Stranger things have happened in Cannock Chase!

Room 2

at Kingsmead

Kingsmead High School in Hednesford, Cannock, is one of the oldest of its type in the local area. Indeed, as boring as it might sound, three generations of my family have attended that school. My father was there in the 1970s, and my grandmother went there in the 1940s when it used to be called "Littleworth School," shortly after it was first opened in 1938. Interestingly, the main building was used to house many evacuees during the Second World War, and that is where the most frequent reports of paranormal activity seem to originate.

For decades now, children who attend Kingsmead school have been terrified about taking lessons in room 2. It has a long history of strange goings-on, but students at the school, and even some teachers, believe the room to be haunted by a little wartime evacuee boy who never found his way home.

The trouble is, this spirit seems very angry about that fact, and as students have come to understand, those unlucky enough to have lessons in room 2 for more than a single term rarely come out unscathed.

During my own time at the school in the early 2000s, I became aware of several ghost stories and legends associated with room 2. I didn't believe them at the time, but my skepticism would soon slap me in the face one morning right before an English lesson.

I walked into the school near the entrance by room 1 and headed up the corridor towards room 4, where I was expected for a maths lesson. As the astute among you readers will reason, that meant I had to walk past the dreaded "room 2." I did so with the utmost haste as, even though I didn't believe the stories, I wasn't the type of teenager to take unnecessary risks.

I'd almost cleared the last window of room 2 when I saw something abnormal out of the corner of my eye. While I might not have been one for taking risks, I was a curious young person, and so I had to stop to check it out. To my utter amazement, sitting at a desk inside the classroom, was a boy no older than eleven wearing what looked like late 1930s period clothing.

I'd seen similar stuff when watching the Nicholas Lyndhurst show "Goodnight Sweetheart" on my TV only a few nights before.

I moved closer to the glass to get a better look at the boy, and he suddenly lifted his head and turned it in my direction. The next thing I knew, a teacher bumped into me and knocked the school books I was holding onto the floor. I picked them up as quickly as possible, but when I climbed back up to my feet, the boy in the classroom was gone.

I believe I saw the ghost two more times after that, but neither occasion was quite as dramatic. Many other people who were at the school at the same time as me also have similar stories.

To my best knowledge, sightings of the ghost in room 2 at Kingsmead largely died down in the years following my departure from the school. At least, that was what I thought until I received the following report from a student who will remain unnamed due to their age:

Dear Mr Brickley,

I go to the same school you went to, and I found your book "UFOs, Werewolves & the Pigman" in our library the other day.

I never knew there was so much weird stuff happening around here, thanks for writing the book!

I actually wanted to tell you about something that happened to me at school last week. If you think I'm silly, that's okay, but I promise I'm telling the truth.

So I have English lessons every Tuesday and Thursday in the same room, and I've started noticing spooky things happening in there. Sometimes my pencil case will move on its own across my table and drop on the floor for instance. I swear I've also seen a small boy sitting under the teacher's desk, but whenever I go and have a look, there is nobody there. Last week things went to a totally new level.

I stayed after class to copy down some work from the whiteboard, and I was the only person still in the room at the time. I heard a rustling sound coming from one of the teacher's cupboards, and so I opened it up to see if it was a rat or something, but it wasn't. I couldn't find what was making the noise so I shut the cupboard, but as I turned around someone slapped me across the face. It really hurt but I was the only person in the room. I started to run for the door and then I was tripped by something on the floor. When I got back to my feet I looked behind me and there was nothing there.

I've had to ask my mum to go to the school and ask if I can change English sets so I don't have to go back in that room, I'm so scared. I think something was after me!

I got in touch with the student and her parents to make sure everyone was okay about the incident, and although her mother and father are a little skeptical, they clearly believe something scared their daughter that day.

I didn't really need to ask the girl, but when I inquired as to which room in the school she was referring to, her answer was predictably *"room 2."*

Ghost on

Platform 1

Cannock Train station is located on the Lichfield Road, and it is an excellent transport hub offering services as far as Rugeley and Birmingham New Street. While the station itself is quite small, it can get very busy in the mornings and around 5pm when people finish work. A lot of local teens use the trains to get to college because the one in Cannock was shut down by the government around ten years ago when the town switched from a Labour to a Conservative constituency.

There have been many eerie sightings at Cannock train station over the years, and a lot of people believe the entire area is haunted by the spirit of a man who threw himself under a train many years ago. As is often the case with suicides, his spirit doesn't seem to be able to find a place to rest, and so he is often seen by locals in the evening time, at around 8pm, standing on platform 1.

The man is always dressed in a long coat, and he wears a porkpie hat on his head. Commuters who catch a glimpse of him often claim he moves erratically, staring at his watch and leaning forwards over the platform to look for an oncoming train. He usually disappears from view after a couple of minutes according to most of those who encounter him, and up until a few months ago, I believed he was a docile spirit, somehow lost between this world and the next, forever replaying the moment he jumped. However, that all changed when I received the following letter from a local lady called Janice:

Hi there Lee!

My friend told me to get in touch with you because I had a really hairy experience a few days ago when I was waiting for the train to Birmingham from Cannock. I saw this guy standing at the end of the platform in the shadows, he looked panicked in some way, and so I went over to see if he needed any help. As I got closer, I could see he was shaking and mumbling something incoherent to himself. I asked if there was anything I could do or anyone I could call.

That's when he turned to face me, and shot forwards towards me so fast that I stumbled and fell down onto the track. I was lucky there was another guy sitting in the shelter because he ran straight over and picked me up off the track before the train arrived. The mumbling guy had vanished by the time I got back on the platform, and I asked the guy who saved me where the other fellow went, but he said he didn't see anyone.

I know this is a bit weird, but I honestly think I startled a ghost. The guy on the platform who shot towards me didn't seem to run, he seemed to glide, and it was almost like he went straight through me. Have you ever heard about anything like this happening before?

I had. I heard stories like that all the time, the only difference was, this was the first occasion on which someone could have been fatally injured because of the ghost on platform 1.

Janice's story has circulated around the Cannock Chase area, and now most people are aware that leaving the spirit alone is a sensible move. But just in case there are any people out there who do attempt to communicate with the phantom, it's worth remembering that he doesn't like to be startled.

The Haunted Toilets

Most people are unaware of this fact, but in Cannock town centre, at the end of the bowling green, there are two toilets that have remained hidden from sight for more than twenty years. You would not know they are there if you go looking for them today, and that is because they were bricked up in the early 1990s, never to be seen again.

The toilets are technically under the end of the bowling green where there is now a bandstand of sorts. There were originally two entrances, one each side of the bandstand, and both had steps down to the toilets underneath. While the local council claims the toilets were bricked up forever to prevent drug use and crime happening down there, I've met many people from Cannock Chase who have a different explanation.

The toilets themselves once played host to a terrible murder that goes unsolved to this day.

Allegedly, a local man walked down the stairs to use the toilets one evening after having a few beers in the Royal Oak pub just opposite. An hour later, someone else walked into the toilets and found his body. The man was lying on the floor with a broken neck and blood seeping out of his mouth. Police investigating the crime determined it was definitely murder, but they never found the culprit. Could that be because the crime had paranormal roots? Quite possibly.

I've spoken to a few locals who tell stories about seeing what they describe as an "old hag" standing behind them when they stood at the urinals in those toilets. They would often see her in the mirror and almost injure their neck from swinging their heads around so fast, but she was never there. They only ever saw her behind them in the mirror. According to one man who contacted me, she would sometimes reach forwards with her haggered fingers as if she was going to grab the back of their necks.

Is it possible she finally made contact on the evening in question and twisted the man's neck? Maybe.

The entire thing was hushed up by local authorities, and the murder recieved very little coverage.

However, within a couple of weeks, the toilets were bricked up, and nobody was ever allowed to go down there again. They weren't filled in entirely though, and the space under the bandstand still exists today. I dread to think what might be down there.

During my investigation into this phenomena, I also spoke to a gentleman who had a fascinating story about the time those toilets were constructed. He told me a weird old homeless woman who used to live in Cannock town centre fell down the hole where the toilets were being built, broke her neck, and died. Apparently, local people celebrated her death as they thought it helped to "clean up the town."

Maybe her evil spirit remains down there today just waiting for the chance to capture another victim?

There's Something Outside the Tent

While wild camping is largely illegal in England, and so pitching your tent on Cannock Chase is a little brave, lots of people choose to do that every year. Many of those people get in touch with me shortly after their camping adventure to let me know about the spooky things that happened, and more often than not, most say they will never dare return to the Cannock Chase woods.

In my other books, I got into detail about the different monsters and aliens spotted in the forest over the years. I imagine many people reading this right now will have read extensively about the Pigman, the black-eyed child, werewolves, the black panther, and many other creatures often spotted between the trees, but this is a book of ghost stories, and so that is where I will focus this section.

In the summer of 2017, I opened my inbox to find this email from a couple of lads who made the mistake of spending a night in their tent on Cannock Chase:

Yo Lee,

I never believed any of the weird stuff about Cannock Chase before, but last night my mate and I had the worst experience ever camping on the Chase.

We pitched our tent just off the Penkridge road in a cool place I know, and we sat out the front eating snacks and having a little smoke. At about 10pm it got dark, and so we got into the tent and zipped ourselves inside. We never sleep much when we camp, and so we spent the next few hours just chatting in our sleeping bags.

By 1am I was starting to get cold, and so I grabbed a jumper from my bag and put it on. Just as I did that we both heard this weird noise coming from outside our tent. It sounded like someone moaning. Have you ever seen Frankenstein? You know the sound the monster makes? It was like that! It scared us to death!

We both froze and stayed silent, just trying to work out what must have been outside of the tent. Then it happened.

A hand was pressed onto the fabric of our tent, and it was huge. It was definitely the hand of a very large man. That was all I could take, and so I unzipped the tent and we both ran to my car and got inside. I turned the headlights on and, sure enough, there was the figure of a shadowy man dressed in Victorian clothing right by our tent. I tried to flash my lights to get his attention, but the second I flicked the lever, the figure disappeared.

We were pretty shook up, and so we didn't fancy spending the rest of the night outside in the woods. We packed up our stuff and swiftly headed back towards the main road. As I was driving out of the little clearing and onto the road, we saw the same figure appear in front of us. I looked at my friend and he said "fuck it man, just drive," so I did. I drove straight ahead towards the figure, and then straight through it! When I looked in the rear-view mirror, I could see the man was still standing there as if he passed right through my car.

A few months after I received that report, I had another one handed to me by the postman:

Hello Mr Brickley,

My wife and I recently spent a night at a hotel in Cannock Chase, and we encountered something rather odd during an evening stroll. Our hotel was right at the edge of the forest, and the landlord told us there was a nice short route we could follow if we wanted to go for a walk and take in some of the views. We thought that was a fantastic idea, but now I wish we'd stayed in our room.

It was probably about seven o'clock when we left the hotel and made our way towards the recommended path. The sun was just going down and the sky looked stunning. It was red and orange, and complemented greatly by the beautiful forest scenery. All seemed peaceful and well until my wife noticed something strange in the distance. There appeared to be a woman bending down, as if she was looking for something on the floor. The unusual thing was, she didn't seem to be solid. We couldn't see her feet, and I swear I could see the trees directly behind her. She looked like a ghost.

My wife insisted we move in her direction, so we did. As we got closer to her position, the woman straightened up before letting out the most otherworldly noise. It was a hellish scream that made both myself and my wife begin to shake. Then she spoke, or rather, shouted "THESE ARE MY WOODS!" at about a million decibels.

We both turned and ran in the opposite direction back to the hotel where we were staying. I told the landlord what had happened and he told me not to worry as we had probably just encountered "the dutchess." I asked who that was and he informed me she was the wife of an old landowner from a couple of hundred years ago. Apparently she has chosen to spend eternity laying her claim to the forest and scaring all those who dare enter it.

I told the landlord that I thought perhaps it would be wise to inform his guests about this prior to sending them off into the woods in future, and I asked why he didn't say anything. The landlord just said "well you wouldn't have believed me without seeing her for yourself," and he was probably right.

The woods of Cannock Chase are a dangerous place for many reasons. There are old mine shafts, the occasional unexploded World War Two bomb, and some of the only venomous snakes in the UK, but local people know none of those things compare to the threat posed by its paranormal inhabitants. This is one portal area that never ceases to amaze.

The Phantom Tip Rat

Cannock landfill site, or "tip" as locals call it, is a huge waste disposal centre in the middle of the town. It has been used for decades to bury all the rubbish inhabitants of Cannock throw away, and as anyone who's ever worked there knows, it can also be a great place to get free stuff. Lots of people throw valuable items away, and those who work at the site often sneakily take it home.

One such worker who used to do that in the 1970s was Terry. He loved his job working at the "tip," and he enjoyed all the bonuses his role had to offer. Indeed, he used to boast in the pub that he kitted out his entire house with things other people had thrown away. Unfortunately, due to alcoholism, Terry lost his job at the tip and eventually died a lonely man a few years later. However, since that time, many workers who finish late at the Cannock landfill site have reported seeing ghostly apparitions of a man that matches Terry's description.

The encounters often happen during the evening time, and so members of the public have rarely reported anything. It is usually the night team or the security staff. They often report seeing an old man wearing a long Parka coat with a big hood sneaking into the landfill site and going through some of the skips. They say he spends around half an hour there looking around, and then walks back off the way he came.

I questioned some of the people who made these reports about whether or not they think it could be a real man breaking into the site, but they all had the same answer for me. They said that if it were a real man, he wouldn't be able to walk straight through the fence. Indeed, it seems that the figure doesn't climb a gate or scale a telegraph pole to break into the landfill site. Instead, people working there have observed him walk straight through a metal fence.

Almost all of the people I spoke to about the sightings at Cannock tip say they are 100% convinced the figure they see on an almost weekly basis is Terry, and they're certain of that because there is a photograph of the man in their office. Apparently it's been there for many years as the image was taken at the first awards ceremony ever held by the company, and you can just about see Terry in the background.

The foreman at the landfill site, who is the only one still working there who met Terry before he died, said to me *"Terry was a tip rat when he worked here, and he continued to break into the site long after he got the sack. We caught him a few times back in the day, climbing over the fence so he could get in and see if there was anything of value he could take him. It doesn't really surprise me that he's carried on doing that after death. He was always a stubborn man."*

If you dare go near Cannock tip at night, and you happen to bump into Terry the phantom tip rat, it would be wise to keep a safe distance. From what I hear, anyone who tries to disturb him gets bin bags thrown in their direction.

Final Word

Well, that about does it for this book about the ghosts of Cannock Chase. If you made it this far, you are no doubt under the impression that Cannock Chase is one of the weirdest and most unusual places in the entire world...and you're right!

My inbox is always open to people who have strange or otherworldly paranormal encounters anywhere in the UK, and as before, you can contact me at:

leebrickleyauthor@gmail.com

Following the publication of this book, I will be taking a break from investigating and reporting on the supernatural events happening in the Cannock Chase area. I've been following the sightings for more than ten years, and it's time I did something else for a little while. Maybe I'll begin investigating cases a little further afield if my services are required. Who knows? I do have somewhat of a passion for haunted hotels, so perhaps I'll write about those in the future.

I wanted to take the opportunity to thank everyone for purchasing the three books detailing my investigation into Cannock Chase, and I hope you will continue to follow my work in the future. I must also extend my thanks to paranormal authors Nick Redfern, Nick Pope, Brad Steiger, and all the others who have helped me along on my journey.

As is often the case with paranormal portal areas, after more than ten years on the scene, I walk away with more questions than answers, but that doesn't really matter to me. The supernatural world is fascinating, and I will always find myself drawn to it, wherever I may end up.

Signing off from Cannock Chase

Your friend

Lee

Other books by this author...

UFOs, Werewolves, & The Pig-Man

Available from AMAZON

The Black-Eyed Child of Cannock Chase

Available from AMAZON

Thanks for reading!

Printed in Great Britain
by Amazon

87326176R00063